Upon Departure

By John Roedel

John Roedel

Upon Departure by John Roedel

Copyright © 2022, John Roedel
All rights reserved. No portion of this book may be reproduced in any form without permission from the publisher, except as permitted by U.S. copyright law. For permissions contact: johnroedel@gmail.com

Author Website: www.johnroedel.com

Cover photo by golden_designs1
www.fiverr.com/golden_designs1

ISBN: 9798439172955

printed in the USA

I am profoundly honored to dedicate this book to the Flournoy family. Tiffany, Dirk, Payton, Bailey, and Isabella, you have given our world a masterclass in how to turn abject heartbreak and grief into something so incredibly beautiful.

Your family is proof that love never dies - it just changes forms. Thank you for showing me how to transform each of my tears into a wildflower seed.

Shine on, Little Moon. Shine On.

John Roedel

The phone rang and my heart sank like a rock.

Ring. Ring. Ring.

Everything was about to change.

Despite my lack of psychic ability, I knew immediately who was calling before I answered. I have found that whenever a loved one is near death the tone coming from a phone seems to sound a little differently. It reverberates with destiny. I can feel the echo of the ring in my rib cage. It's like the trumpet of an angel.

I had just come home from the hospital after a grueling 10-hour shift watching my father straddle the wafer line between this physical life and the Great Beyond. When I left him, all indications suggested that my dad's condition was stable. It seemed like it was the perfect time to sneak back to my apartment in order to reacquaint myself with my bed and shower.

However, on my way out the door, one of his kind nurses advised me that they would "call me right away" if his condition worsened.

"Okay, but you don't see that happening tonight, right?" I asked. In hindsight, it was more of a plea than a question.

"The only thing I know about these things is that they never keep a set schedule or act predictably," she said ominously as she squeezed my shoulder warmly.

Her words caused the skin on my upper back to crawl.

I wanted (needed) to hug her, but figured I should probably attempt to maintain the border between a healthcare professional and a brokenhearted son who was facing the death of someone he loved for the very first time in his life. So, I smiled wearily and began my exhausting shuffle through the long hospital corridor, down the rickety elevator and into the parking garage where I had parked my sad excuse of a car a half-a-day earlier.

Before going back to my apartment, I stopped by my childhood house where my mom and dad had lived since the early 1970s. My older brother was also temporarily residing there at the time. He had raced across the country from California a few days earlier to return to our home in Wyoming when my father's battle against lung cancer had taken a dire turn.

John Roedel

My mom and brother were also recovering from their long shift at the hospital. They had left my dad's bedside about 40-minutes before I did - and they looked as emotionally spent as I felt.

We had all been holding a vigil next to him for days and it was starting to break us down. Nobody ever had told me how debilitating it is to watch a beloved slowly transform into air and light.

The three of us sat around our oval kitchen table in silence. This table was used to four Roedels being gathered around it. We were all situated in our usual spots. My brother was sitting at 9 o'clock, my mom at noon, and I was positioned in my customary 6 o'clock position.

My dad's empty chair loomed like a comet in the night sky. I couldn't take my eyes off of it. His vacant space felt like a coming apocalypse.

We sat together without speaking for a while longer before I stood up to go to my apartment across town. I knew I needed to get a couple of hours of sleep before resuming my place next to my father's beeping monitors and whirling machines.

"I'll see you in the morning," I said to my mom and brother as I fumbled with my car keys.

"Make sure you answer the phone if you get called," my mom told me.

"I doubt we will hear anything tonight," I replied.

My mom frowned.

"Just answer it."

It only took me ten minutes to drive my cheap car to my cheap apartment. Within moments of walking through the door, I poured myself into bed in anticipation that I would quickly be deep asleep. However, despite how truly bone-tired I was, slumber never came.

My body was out of batteries - but my heart and mind were a roaring wildfire of anxiety, guilt, and relentless pangs of intense invisible pain that felt like it was radiating from the very mantle of my being.

I sprawled out on my bed for an hour transfixed by the ceiling fan whipping and rattling above me. My apartment did not handle the stuffy Wyoming July air and I constantly had the fan set on the highest possible setting which made the dusty blades look like a blur. I observed that if I started up into the whirling motion of the fan for a long period of time

John Roedel

that my eyes would start to play tricks on me. I began to see memories of my dad and me together play out in stop motion through the rotating swirl of the moving blades.

My dad and I snowmobiling together in
Steamboat Springs, Colorado, when I was eight years old.
My hands wrapped around his waist.
Our faces frozen with a mixture of snow and smiles.

I'm now a teenager. The two of us standing barefoot together in a river together with fishing pools in our hands. The water moving around us.
Both of us casting
and reeling our lines out under the winking glow of a rising
summer moon.

The look on my dad's face as I delivered a near-perfect commencement speech
at my high school graduation. I was killing it and his face beamed with a pride I had never seen before.

Watching my dad work his magic from behind a pharmacy counter just a couple of weeks earlier. A woman had come in and asked for some help paying for her medication and despite how miserable my dad felt he sat on the phone unsuccessfully debating with her insurance company for 45 minutes. Eventually, he just paid for her prescription himself. I remember how the woman hugged him at the end - and how pale his face looked - and how he hid how much pain he was from her as she squeezed him.

Memories like these kept playing like a silent film amid the rambling fan blades above me. With each passing image, I could feel the levy that was keeping all of my tears at bay begin to break inside of me. Watching my dad begin to pack his proverbial bags for the afterlife over the past few days had broken me in ways I could have never imagined before - but despite all of that, I hadn't cried yet.

I was afraid that if I started crying I would never be able to stop. I was afraid of this rising terror inside of me that my father, who was the North Star in my life, would soon fall into a black hole. I was afraid that my dad was about to go somewhere I would never be able to follow.

I was so afraid. Then it happened.....*of course, it happened....*

The phone rang and my heart sank like a rock.

John Roedel

Upon Departure 7

Despite my lack of psychic ability, I knew who was calling before I had to answer it. Whenever a loved one is near death it seems like the tone of the ringtone sounds a little differently. You can feel the echo of it in your rib cage. It's like the trumpet of an angel.

I reached over to my nightstand and pulled the phone off of the receiver and brought it up to my ear.

"Hello, this is John," I answered as if I was expecting a call from a business associate.

"John, this is one of your father's nurses at the hospital." a woman quietly said.

I waited a fat moment before responding. I knew what she was going to say. I was certain that this was about to be a conversation would remember for the rest of my life.

Eventually, I cleared my throat and replied:

"Uh, huh."

"You need to get back here right away. He doesn't have very much time left."

Within moments I was back in my car speeding across town to get to the hospital. The whole frantic drive has been recorded on the DVR of my heart. I can remember everything so vividly. My hands gripping the worn-out wheel of my car. The way I looked in the mirror whenever I caught a glimpse of myself. My hair was in full bird's nest mode. I looked homeless. The radio playing Pink Floyd's "Comfortably Numb".

The stars above were blazing and twinkling as if they were auditioning for the next Wyoming Chamber of Commerce newsletter.

Of course, I hit every single red light possible in my race to try and see my dad one last time before he slipped across the veil. With each hard stop, I imported whoever was the Patron Saint of Small Town Infrastructure to intervene and get the traffic lights still ahead of me to cooperate.

"Come on! Come on! COME ON!" I screamed at each red light while rocking back and forth in my seat as if I was sitting on an active hive of mutated hornets.

John Roedel

Getting from my apartment to where my father was taking his last breaths usually only took about nine minutes. However, by the time I saw the outline of the hospital in the darkened skyline, it felt like I had been driving for twelve hours.

> I had to get there in time.
> I had to get there before it was too late.
> I had so much left to say.

I was so angry at cancer - but I reserved my true rage for myself. Every thought that sped through my mind was an indictment against my heart for all of the times I had let my dad down in the past.

Why did I go home in the first place? I should have stayed there. I shouldn't have left him. How could I have left? I am such a bad son. I never was able to make him proud of me. I am such a bad son. Why am I not there! Why are these lights all red!!

I was a block away from the hospital when I got stopped at the final red light that stood between me and my father. At this point, I was in full panic attack mode. I found it very difficult to control my breathing. It felt like I was trapped inside of a collapsed mine shaft. Despite being under a wide-open Wyoming blinking near-midnight sky I had this sensation that I was being buried alive.

"Let's go! Let's Go!" I begged the stoplight.

It didn't reply. In fact, it seemed like the light was taking so much longer than all of the other asshole lights I had encountered on my drive across town. I started banging my hands on the steering wheel and screaming this guttural cry that I don't think I would ever be able to reproduce again in my life.

That's when it happened - the only supernatural moment I can ever remember happening to me in my life.

In the midst of my radiating rage and panic there came this wave of peace that seemed like emitted from outside of me. It was like a wave. It was like a blanket. It was like the way a warm sunbeam catches the bare nape of our neck during a cool spring morning.

The best way I can describe what I experienced is that I felt held by invisible arms. Something was wrapping itself around my convulsing body. I was a wildfire of unhinged emotion that was being put out by an unseen downpour of love and comfort.

John Roedel

Suddenly instead of screaming at the red light or letting the cruelest of thoughts whip me over and over - I felt something else.

I felt harmony. I felt at peace. I felt comfort. I knew right then and there that my dad had gone. I looked down at the flickering green clock on my radio console. The time was 11:13 P.M.

"It's okay," I whispered to myself. "It's all going to be okay."

With that, the light changed from red to green. This time, instead of shoving my foot down on the accelerator like a stunt driver in a remake of Cannonball Run, I just took a deep breath and applied some light pressure to the pedal. I was certain that there was no reason to hurry anymore.

I drove up to the third floor of the hospital garage, parked my car, and slowly started to make my way into the building. The normal bustle of the hospital was absent as I ambled through the lobby and toward the elevator.

I had spent a few overnight shifts over the past week and never got used to how terrifying the complex was at night. All of those horror movies I watched as a kid made the near-empty hospital hallways a bit unsettling for my sensitive heart. However, this time, I didn't feel that creeping sense that a knife-wielding psycho was lurking in the shadows.

This time, I could feel a different presence. The wave of peace that had enraptured me in the car had followed me into the hospital. I sweat that I felt like a hand was on my shoulder.

I rode the shaky elevator up to the third floor where my dad's room was. As the door opened I saw a group of nurses standing outside of his room in a semi-circle. Once I walked through the door, they all slowly turned their heads toward me in perfect synchronization. I was sure they had to have practiced that. It was so precise.

Their faces shared the exact expression that confirmed what I had already inexplicably come to know while I was driving to the hospital - my dad, Andrew Roedel, who had been my constant, had been swept away by eternity.

The same nurse who I spoke to before I left his room earlier, strode toward me quickly and gave me the hug I so wanted earlier. "I'm sorry, John. I'm so sorry. He's gone. It was so peaceful, but he's gone. It just happened a few minutes ago. I'm so sorry." she said to me softly while wrapping her arms around my neck.

John Roedel

"It's okay. It's all going to be okay." I said in a repeat of the exact lines I had uttered to myself at the final stoplight.

She informed me that I was the first of my family members to arrive. Then, after a quick squeeze, the nurse ended her kind embrace that I would have likely allowed it to go on for a month if it were up to me. She stepped out of my way so I could walk into his room. I braced myself for what I was about to experience and then I went inside.

Before that moment. I had never seen a body without a soul inside of it. I didn't know what to expect, but this wasn't it.

It was like walking past a vacant downtown store.
It was like looking at a hole in the ground where a redwood tree used to stand.
It was like trying to read a book that was only a cover.
The whole room had an empty cocoon vibe to it.

My dad was truly gone.

I remember how silent the room was. All of the beeping monitors and whiling medical devices had been silenced. It was as noiseless as space. His hospital room had become a sacred chapel of hushed grace.

I sat at his bedside for a moment and uttered a few promises in his ear that I hoped his spirit was still able to listen through. I assured him that I would take care of our mom and our family drug store. I swore that I would never forget how many sacrifices he made for me during my life. I spent those few moments saying and singing every unspoken word I should have said while we were both upright.

Then it happened...*of course, it happened....*

Once I stopped pouring out my heart to my day, the emotional levy inside of me broke open. It was like an ancient damn that finally gave way to 100,000 years of river water that had been trying to push through. Tears started gushing out of me unlike ever before. The strange thing was that I didn't even know I was crying until I felt teardrops plop on the hand that I used to hold my dad's face. I wasn't heaving, moaning or sobbing. It was the quietest form of weeping possible.

Apparently, my tears had picked up on the holy and silent vibe of the room, and decided to follow suit.

John Roedel

Within a few seconds, my cheeks were covered in a flood of tears. I was uncontrollably pushing out every single tear that I had been holding onto. My face was drenched in salt and memory.

My mom and brother soon arrived at my dad's room to discover that he had already flown away with the angels. I saw their heartbreak cross over their face in the same slow motion that mine did. The seemingly endless tears began to flow for them as well. Between the three of us, I am surprised we didn't turn the entire floor into a stream. My mother and brother each spent time saying every single word that they needed to say to this man who had been the spine of our family's book.

"What are we going to do now?" my mom asked me.

"It's okay. It's all going to be okay," I said for the third time in the past 20-minutes. Turns out, this was my new mantra. I wasn't even sure if I believed it - but every time I said these words I felt better.

By the time we left the hospital room, we were met by a group of extended family members and friends who were standing outside in the hallway. Each person gave us a deep hug and gave us a foreshadowing of the conversations we would be having over and over for the next month:

"I can't believe he is gone."

"I'm so sorry."

"He is in a better place."

"Please let us know if we can do anything."

At this point, I was a full-on wreck. For the first time in my life, I didn't feel self-conscious crying in front of other people. Even if I did, there was no stopping it. The tears had not relented in their need to escape my body. I have no idea how my body was able to keep this production up due to how little water I consumed on a daily basis.

At the end of the gauntlet of well-wishers I was obliged to pass through was one of our family's most stoic members. This gentleman was a bull in human clothing. He was the kind of guy who would probably go out and mow the lawn an hour after having his leg bitten off by a gator. He is the kind of iron-jawed cowboy that turns heads.

John Roedel

He took me aside and shook my hand in a manner that suggested he was trying to turn my wee knuckles into a delicious breakfast jam. He then put his hands on my shoulders and stared down at me and said:

"The time for crying is over. You need to bury those tears and be strong for your mom. She can't see you like this," he said to me sternly while handing me a couple of kleenexes.

Normally, when an elder gives me a piece of unsolicited advice I nod my head and act like I'm absorbing it earnestly. I am not a creature who enjoys debate - so, often I am happy to seem like I'm complying for the sake of ending the conversation as quickly as possible. Not this time. This time, my typical defenses were down and I spoke freely. Instead of surrendering to his appeal, I stepped back from my well-intended relative and sharply replied:

"I won't do that."

He didn't respond verbally, but I could see that he know had decided that I was being hysterical.

"These tears are proof," I said.

"Of what?" he asked.

"That I loved him."

On my drive home from the hospital to my dingy apartment, I made every single light.

The Poetry of Grief

Everyone has a story similar to the one I just shared. Nothing I wrote is unique to the human experience. One of the most heartbreakingly beautiful things about being alive is that our physical bodies are so temporary. This means, of course, that all of the relationships we make with one another here on Earth are soundtracked by the noise of an hourglass pushing sand from one end to the other.

I'm writing this book as the COVID-19 Pandemic appears to be heading toward another lull that I pray will ensure it will be the last time we hear from it for a long while. What the past few years have reminded me is that death doesn't care what your tax

John Roedel

bracket is or how many church services you attend. Death is indiscriminate and it will eventually come to stamp each of our celestial passports.

Walking into the deep forest of grief is something we all must do. It's a universal rite of passage. Over the last couple of years, however, it seems as if we have all been asked to spend more time in Grief Woods than we could have ever imagined.

Being mortal means that we are all caught in a loop of meeting each other at Baggage Claim, falling in love with each other, and then slowly walking with each other to our unannounced Departure Gate.

It's the bittersweet cycle of what happens when we give our hearts to another:

1) We meet someone.
2) We grow close.
3) We allow roots to become entangled with them.
4) We depend on this person.
5) We have to say goodbye.
6) We grieve.
7) We reunite again in the place where we trade our skin in for light.

All of that seems pretty straightforward to me - except #6. To grieve the death of a beloved isn't something that we check off of a box. Once we experience grief it changes us forever. Grief transforms us. Grief doesn't just stay for a weekend. Grief moves into the loft in our hearts. Grief isn't a hitchhiker we pick up on the roadside. Grief becomes the driver.

My father passed away over 20-years ago and there isn't a day that passes where I don't relive his last few days. I don't have a great memory - but I can remember what those last sacred days of his were like as if they just unfolded in front of me for the first time.

My dad's death was my first brush with mortality, but it hasn't been my last.

John Roedel

I have had plenty of other encounters with death as I've been forced to say goodbye to my mom, friends, and other family members who I loved with every fiber of my being. Every time I lose someone to the Great Mystery I find myself surprised all over again by how the grief that follows affects me.

Grief is more than sadness and despair. Sometimes grief is laughter as I recall a hilarious story from our past. Other times grief is regret as I lament over all of the words I left unsaid between us. Grief isn't one emotion. Grief encompasses all of them.

Grief isn't an obstacle we overcome- it's a masterclass in what it means to be human.

This is a poetry collection that honors our grief as a natural wonder that terraforms the landscape of our world in increments. It can take a lifetime to find peace when our loved one becomes an empty chair at our kitchen table.

These poems are a pushback against this fast-forward world of quick fixes and insta-healing world we all live in. So much pressure is put on us to "go back to normal" after our hearts are broken by death. There is this unspoken call for us to have our wounds become scars long before they are ready to. The pieces in this collection of poetry are anchored around the concept that grief isn't something we "get over" or "overcome".

Experiencing grief is a bit like watching a coral reef slowly develop in the ocean. It can look a little different every day. It can change its color and appearance over time. Grief isn't a passage that we walkthrough. Grief is a natural wonder that we are called to sit and experience.

This collection asks the reader to not hide from their grief - but to let it grow instead. We don't bury our grief in the darkness. We pour as much light on it as we can and watch it become something beautiful.

Just like a coral reef.

John Roedel

Coral reefs grow when they have access to light. It changes their color. The light transforms them from underwater rocks into something that we can see from an airplane.

These poems don't offer a prescription to overcome our grief. What I do ask is for you to consider our ability to grieve for one another as a bittersweet lifelong wonder rather than a curse. To grieve means that we have taken the risk to love without fear.

My hope is that this collection on grief will invite you to sit with your heartbreak for as long as it takes it to form a relationship with it.

My own relationship with grief began in July of 1997 and we have been going strong since. I haven't really stopped crying since that day when a slew of red lights caused me to miss my father's departure from Earth.

Each of these poems that follow is a single teardrop of grief I have shed over the course of my life. I would be honored if you helped me catch them.

"These tears are proof."

"Of what?"

"That I loved."

John Roedel

Upon Departure 16

Prologue

here is a piece
of my heart

~ please take it

not as a souvenir
but rather, as a deposit

to ensure that no matter
the distance or the dimension

that may separate us

I will come back to you
to make myself whole again

John Roedel

#1

I don't care what form
you return to me
I just want you back

If you come back to me
as rain

    I'll sit under your downpour and
become drenched in the memory
of how we first met

If you come back to me
as a western breeze

    I'll lay down in a field and make a
hundred-thousand wishes as you blow
dandelion seeds all over me

If you come back to me
as a cloud

    I'll climb the highest peak just to
let you wrap me up in your
misty-morning arms

If you come back to me
as our favorite song on the radio

    I'll pull the car over immediately
and let the music retell our love story
one 80's power ballad at a time

If you come back to me
as an eagle feather

    I'll let you tickle the inside
of my fingers the way you
used to whenever we held hands

If you come back to me

John Roedel

as a light peeking through the trees

    I'll stop walking to watch you all day long
as you dance wildly among the pine needles
until your glow is claimed by the horizon

If you come back to me
as a hummingbird

    I will listen so quietly as you
Whisper all the secrets of
The afterlife in my ear

If you come back to me
as a row of goosebumps on my bare arm

    I will trace my fingers across my skin
Carefully so I can read the love letter
You wrote to me in spirit braille

If you come back to me
as a single fat teardrop

    I will close my eyes
As you bless the tip of
My nose with your kiss of peace

If you come back to me
as a twinkling star in the night sky

    I will renounce my allegiance
To gravity so I can rise
Up into space and orbit you

If you come back to me
As a roaring campfire

    I will stand so close to you
That the smoke of your presence
Lingers in my hair for weeks

If you come back to me

    John Roedel

As the summer

    I will fall asleep in the heat of
your green garden promises
you make me with your hot July breath

If you come back to me
as the Winter

    I will exhale so deeply
So I can watch you
Draw pictures with my frozen breath

If you come back to me
As a flower

    I will ask God to cash
in my available credit and
Turn me into your honeybee

If you come back to me
As a picture in my phone

    I will pinch my eyes so tightly
it causes me to time travel right to that
moment so I can tell you everything I never said

If you come back to me
As a dream

    I will put as many dream rocks in my
Pockets as I can to keep me from
Floating straight up through my eyelids

If you come back to me
As a stretching strand of lightning

    I will stand outside
And wait for your thunder
To shake the cobwebs off of my heart

If you come back to me

                  John Roedel

Upon Departure 20

As a heartbeat

   I will place my hand on my wrist
And feel you coursing through
My thin veins

If you come back to me
As a passage in a book

   I will grab the fattest eraser I can find
And get rid of all the periods so you
Can become a run-on sentence

If you come back to me
As an overwhelming wave of grief

   I will let you hold me
In your arms as I
Cry on the floor in the bathroom

If you come back to me
In the eyes of a child

   I will give you a quick
Smile and nod as
You start your adventure all over again

There is no dress code required
  ~ come as you however you are now

No matter how you return to me
I will be waiting

Whether you come back
as a piece of piano music
Or as a heart-shaped cloud

Whether you reveal yourself
As a morning songbird
Or a midnight candle

I'll be paying attention

                        John Roedel

To be a watcher is the joyful work
Of the grieving

And when I see you
Oh, my love,
When I see you again

It will be like you never left

John Roedel

#2

I can't say the word
"afterlife" anymore

at least not in how I was
taught to use it in a sentence

I'm not sure if I even
understand what
the afterlife means

though, it should be
noted that I was (and continue to be)
a terrible Sunday School student

I never concerned myself
with the mysteries of theology
    in fact, I think I was distracted
       on the day a somber sermon on death was
       being given by our parish priest when I was eleven

I think instead of paying attention
to the talk on hellfire and Heaven

I was happily sitting in a pew
at St. Mary's Cathedral writing love
notes on a tithing envelope that I would
later (unsuccessfully) ask the usher
to deliver the girl with tight braids
who sat three rows in front of my family

~ so I know my liturgical flirting
kept me out of the loop when
it came to the dogma of death

but I never really connected
with the idea or concept of an
afterlife no matter what the well-intended
middle-aged man in an alb said

I'm certainly not arguing that

John Roedel

Upon Departure 23

things end for us the moment
we surrender to the cosmic pull
of forever peace

I would argue the
exact opposite occurs
~I think our story rages on

but...just not into an afterlife
that serves as an exclusive nightclub
for the chaste and chronically polite

there is no "after"
         ~there is just life

when the sun turns orange at sunset
and finds itself contorting beams just
for you over the blade of the horizon

it is still the same light

when the piano melody
melts into a violin so the
sound feels like an angel
is kissing your forehead

it is still the same music

and when our heartbeats
for the final time
and we trade our skin
for star-fire

it is the same life

~what does the afterlife even mean?
does it mean beyond?
does it mean separate?
does it mean graduation?

we are cloud, rainwater,
stream, ocean and fog

John Roedel

Upon Departure 24

we become whatever
we need to next

we are the photosynthesis
of grace and wonder

because our lives are a circle
and circles don't have an after
they just keep going
our existence has
always been in a loop

it's an endless
piece of moving art
that completes itself
again and again

and someday when
our bones become spirit
nothing about us will change

no matter our form
~ whether it be skin or shadow

life is life

there can be no after
for something that never ends

which makes this all
such an adventure

John Roedel

#3

Me: Hey God.

God: Hey John.

Me: What should I say to somebody who is about to die?

God: The exact same things you should say to everybody else whenever you have a chance.

Me: What's that?

God: I love you.
       I love you so much.
       I forgive you.
       I'm sorry.
       I'm blessed to know you.
       I'm so grateful to you.
       I think that you are beautiful.
       I can't wait to see you again.
       I love you.
       I love you so much.

****

{we are roommates in hospice care together and every conversation we share

could be the most important moment in our lives}

{you and I are both dying right now so let's not leave a single word unspoken between us ~ let's speak the softest poetry to each other by moonlight

because one of us might not physically be here in the morning}

{we are fading stars calling to each other across the vast universe to bathe each other in the softest light of love one last time

before we slip through the vortex and back into time}

John Roedel

{together we can build a confessional out of the gentle glances we give each other while we hold hands

and quietly pardon every scar we carved into each other before we knew any better}

{if we remember that every heartbeat is being counted then there will never be any ordinary seconds spent between us

~ each breath we share will be draped in importance}

{in this planet of 8 billion hospice patients there is so much magic and so many chances to brush each other with rose petals

before we are swept away by resurrection}

let's lace our hands
as if eternity is opening
up the veil into the Great
Mystery right in front of us

let's feel our fingers against
each other as if this is the
last time we will touch before
we become celestial kites

let's part our lips and say
what we should have said
to each other years ago

I love you.
    I love you so much.
    I forgive you.

I'm sorry.
    I'm blessed to know you.
    I'm so grateful to you.

I think that you are beautiful.
    I can't wait to see you again.
    I love you.

John Roedel

Upon Departure 27

I love you so much.

John Roedel

#4

"I miss you."

"I'm right here next to you"

"But I can't see you."

"Then close your eyes and feel me."

"Oh. There you are."

"Here I am, my love."

your beloved,
~ they aren't gone

~ they are right here

it's just that they have changed forms

it's just that they were the lake that eventually became the rolling thunderhead

it's just that they were the seed that eventually became the lush apple tree

it's just that they were the fistful of wet clay that eventually became the cup of eternity

your beloved,
~they aren't gone

~ they are right here

and they're holding you as you tremble
and they're dancing in the swirling galaxies of tears that are forming in your eyes
and they're whispering your name softly between the silent gaps of your thumping heartbeat

John Roedel

and they're gently blowing on the hairs that are rising on your
arms right now

your beloved,
~they aren't gone

~ they are right here

and they know that you love them still and forever

because love is an endless string of warm sunlit
memories tied between two people
because love is a circle drawn on the wall of time
in permanent red marker

because love is the act of holding hands with
another person and counting to infinity by twos

your beloved
~they aren't gone
~ they are right here

and they are leaving love notes for you everywhere

that over and over and
in a hundred million different ways
say the exact same thing:

"we have not been separated
we have not been separated
we have not been separated"

your beloved
~they aren't gone
~ they are right here

and they want me to tell you something:

they are
so proud
of you

John Roedel

#5

Heaven is a record store
- let me explain,

every kind word
that we say
to each other while
we are alive
is being recorded

by the stylus of
our tongues

onto each other's
smooth hearts

and we'll
show our hearts
off once we all
meet in the
forever place,

which I am
convinced is a
record store

that smells like
musty carpets,
plastic wrap
and memory

then while we
are all there together

sitting on heaven's
slightly worn leather
couches

we'll all have a turn

taking out

John Roedel

our vinyl
hearts

and placing the cosmic
needle on the grooves
that we made in each other

and listen to
all the music that

we made together

play through
the speakers
of heaven

every sweet melody
every kind lyric
we recorded on each other's hearts

is the soundtrack
of eternity

#6

here is a story about you
that I heard from a gossiping angel
who was snacking on a strawberry
in the tree in my backyard this past summer

the angel said that

you used to soar
above the world
they said that

you were once surrounded
by so many miracles
that nobody could tell
where the wonder began and you ended

you were a swirl
of soaring grace
but one day (a long while ago)

a comet came roaring down
and the sky came apart all around you

and after being
so wounded by the fire

you became grounded to gravity
and found yourself wounded and walking
in a foreign land

eventually, you were captured by those
who told you that flying would now be
"too dangerous" for you

they said that
that you would enjoy
the safety of confinement
so, they put you in a cage
and clipped your wings

John Roedel

for "your own safety"

the angel went on to say that

for years you stared through
the iron bars and fantasized about
taking flight once more
~ to feel the great wind in your face
~ to be untethered to earthly things
~ to be able to flirt with heaven again

I heard that you dreamed
every night about being
able to reclaim your freedom
"but your freedom never came,"
the angel told me

and over time,
you fell into a deep despair
"I'll never leave this place," you repeated
to yourself over and over

The angel said that in your
most desperate hour
you prayed for God to let
your heart stop beating

so you could become a ghost
in order to feel yourself become
tangled up in a hot summer breeze

- even if just for a second
I heard that you prayed to Spirit
to allow your suffering to end

Even if that meant that you
would be swept up by oblivion

I began to weep as I listened to your story
because it sounded so familiar

the angel reported somberly that

John Roedel

your prayers were never answered

and you resigned yourself
to being stuck in the cage forever

then the angel said that
during one winter night
(not too long ago)
a moonbeam winked at you
through the gaps of your cage bars

and how overtook you were
by the soft glow

And how you sang a psalm about
how lovely it all was

until the moon heard you
and changed its hue from
white to lavender

and suddenly you remembered
something you were told when
you first hatched

your voice can
change the world

and that

there is no prison
that can hold your song

the angel said that even though
they clipped your wings
and put you in a cage
you let your voice grow feathers
and it slips out through the cage every
night to explore the world

every time you open
your mouth and sing

John Roedel

you escape the prison
that you thought you
would never leave

I heard that you learned
that you didn't need your
wings to be close to heaven
you just needed
to find your voice

and as the angel hugged me goodbye
she told me

that once you started singing
~ you never stopped

and that now you are surrounded
by so many miracles that nobody can
tell where the wonder begins and you end

you are still such a swirl
of soaring grace

oh, my love,
as the strawberry scented
angel rose up I shouted

how I couldn't wait to hear
your song

because

maybe it will
help me find
the way out
of my own cage

John Roedel

#7

~ you are standing in the wind
but you are not of the wind

the wind is just what flows through you

~ you are standing in the river
but you are not of the river

the river is just what moves around you

~ you are standing in the sunlight
but you are not of the sunlight

the sunlight is just what passes through you

~ you are standing in the wreckage
but you are not of the wreckage

the wreckage is just what surrounds you

~ you are radiating with joy
but you are not of the joy

the joy is just what moves through you

~ you are suffering from depression
but you are not of the depression

depression is just what passes through you

~ you are so lovely in the skin you were given
but you are not of your skin

your skin is just what surrounds you

~ you are living in this hard world
but you are not of this hard word

this hard world is just what moves around you

John Roedel

my love,
everything
is in constant transition

everything that happens to you
is nomadic

the things of this world are
constantly traveling through you
but it should never become

you

a car doesn't become a part of
the tunnel it races through,
does it?

you are the great passage
where all meaningful
experiences move through

be careful of the things you cling to
or they will define you
or they will jam up the tunnel

let these things come
and let these things go

so you can allow for whatever
needs to come next
safe passage through you

be the hallow bone

~ strong
   ~unblocked
      ~unburdened

nearly weightless

be the gentle pipeline
where the matters of life

John Roedel

move through you so
effortlessly to get to
wherever they need to go next

my love,
we have been wounded
but we are not of our wounds

we have been angry
but we are not of our anger

we have cried a thousand tears
but we are not of our tears

it's all a passage
of emotion and experience

it's the freeway of life

that became a mountain tunnel
welcoming invisible travelers
to pass straight through
the center of our hearts

it's all
coming and going
coming and going
coming and going going going

don't cling to any of it

keep your hands free
so I can wrap mine
in yours

because, if anything is to remain
with us after we leave this world
that we are moving through

let it just be our connection

please, oh please

John Roedel

let it be us

I may not be of
this world

but I am of you

my love,
I am of you

John Roedel

#8

Open up a bag of
Red Rope Licorice

and suddenly I'm
eight years old again.

It's 1982.

I'm standing in
the middle of
our family's old drug store.

The waxy floors
that are only cleaned
every six weeks.

The humming lights
that never quite illuminate
the far corners of our long rectangle shop.

The overfilled bins of kite string
and rows of Russell Stovers chocolate.

The discount birthstone jewelry counter
and the smell of raw film
coming from the camera department.

It's all there.

I'm back.

Really.
This isn't a dream.
I can feel the bag of licorice
against my hairless arms.
I swear it.

I've fallen through a confectionery
wormhole to my past.

John Roedel

Please believe me.

I can see my dad
behind the pharmacy counter.

Smiling.
Always smiling.

Handing a towering red-haired man
a tiny bottle of eggshell pills.

At this age, I don't really know what a pharmacist does. People bring in slips of paper with the worst cursive writing you will ever see and give them to my father so he can transform them into amber-colored vials filled with remedy.

He is a magician.

The red-haired man leaves and
my dad raises his hand to his mouth and
takes a slow drag from his cigarette.

A cigarette that he
got from our store.

A store that had much
tobacco In stock
as we did any medicine
that fought the disease
that came with it.

Our store trafficked in both
the disease and the cure.

My dad, now with
a fresh haze of
smoke that in 15 years would
turn into cancer billowing around him

finds me with his eyes.

I am sixty feet away.

John Roedel

I am 35-years away.

But
I am caught in his gaze
like a fish on a line.

My dad smiles at me.
I am complete.
I live for his smile.

He is my smiling smoking hero
in a lab coat.

He begins to fade
into the smoke.

The store is disappearing below and above me.

I am traveling back.

Before he is obscured by time
and I'm returned back to
my uncomfortable adulthood,

I smile at my dad one last time

As he does at me.
As he does at me.
As he does at me.

We are now shadows to one another.

I take to my Red Ropes.
My dad takes to his smoking.

Our little silent vices each trying
to kill us in their own way.

We finally melt away from each other.

I'm back.
The vision is over.

John Roedel

But my lips still taste like candy.
And my tears smell just like sugar.
And my shirt smells like my dad's smoke.
And my smile is frozen to my face:

You see,

every time I eat red licorice
I fall backward through the calendar
and return to under the leaky roof of my
family's once proud store.

And every single time I time travel
on the wave of crimson delicious sweetness

I am reminded that death
can't
kill our memories.

So, that must
make it powerless.

John Roedel

#9

I woke up
this morning
afraid that I had
begun my last day

so

I tightened the
faucets on all of
the clocks in my house

until every minute
felt like it was a fat
droplet of water
resting on the lip
of a spigot

that it clung to

just before letting go
and splashing on
my bare toes

and now, time is
just dripping by me
in slow motion

my love,

I have discovered
how less scary the
world is when it isn't
pouring through my
fingers all at once

~ when I take life
just one easy
drop at a time

things don't feel

John Roedel

so overwhelming

and I'm
starting to
stare at each
leisurely forming
bead of time

like the unhurried
marvel it is

like the unique
little bulb of
reflected light

it was made to be

and now
I think I
might just
make it
another day

my love,

~when this life
isn't a rushing flood
of blurred moments

it's so damn
beautiful

~when life becomes
a deliberate pitter-patter
of wonderment

it's all exactly
what I imagined
it was going
to be like before
I was born

John Roedel

it's a downpour of
life that comes down
one methodical
drippity drop
of time at a time

drop
I can make it

drop
I can make it

drop
it's all a miracle

drop
it's all such an adventure

drop
I can't wait to see what comes next

drop
thank you, Creation for giving me another day

drop
I can make it
drop
I can make it
drop
oh my love,

drop
I'm not scared anymore

drop
I can see angels in the clouds now

drop
I think I am going to be okay

drop
I can make it

John Roedel

oh, my love, I can make it
dropdropdropdropdrop

#10

your grief
is the purest
love letter
that you can
ever send
to the one
you have lost
to death

                    you can take each
                      memory and
                  cover them in the
                        first-class
                  postage stamps
                  of your deepest
                          longing

and offer them
up to the cosmos
one heartfelt
sob at a time

                        don't fret,
                        my love

                        your letters
                        will get to
                    where they need
                          to go

I have discovered
that angels make
the best mail carriers

they gather up all of your
mournings and missives
with their velvet gloves

                    and fly them
                    straight to

                    John Roedel

the piece of
your heart
that you have
been separated
from

no matter
the light-years
between you
and the one you have
lost

your   bereavement
is always scheduled
for same-day delivery

every   tear
that rolls down
the grooves
on your face
is the most
tender   postcard
you will ever write

and it will always get
to the one you grieve for

and it will say the same thing
as any other postcard:

"Wish You Were Here
- xxoo!"

John Roedel

#11

welcome to the steep edge
of all that you think that you can take

welcome to the point where
where it feels like you're gonna break

welcome to the brick wall that others
have built right in your gentle way

welcome to the debt that others owe
and then try to make you pay

welcome to the spot where
it feels so easy to quit

welcome to where your aching legs
beg for you to finally sit

welcome to the grief that becomes
rooted deep inside all you do

welcome to all of the regrets that
keeps reintroducing itself to you

welcome to the night that feels like
it well never come to an end

welcome to the raging tempest that'd
rather have you snap then to bend

welcome to people who discount your work
with a simple wave of their hand

welcome to a house being built for you
on a shifting pile of clumpy sand

welcome to your gravestone that somebody
already etched in your full birth name

welcome to your public lynching where

John Roedel

everybody knows your secret shame

welcome to your bed where sleep
won't ever seek to come

welcome to a year of winter
without any peaking sun

welcome to the heartbreak that comes
from somebody walking out the door

welcome to your shaking hands that come
when you just can't take any more

welcome to your guilt that refuses to
ever take a vacation day

welcome to a sea of closed ears when you
have something to say

welcome to all the tests
that are written to try
and make you fail

~ welcome to not surrendering
but instead writing on every wall
the word: PREVAIL

everything that is chewing on you
isn't strong enough to cut
your skin

everything that is trying to break
you down is destined to
never win

you are patched together with
tiger blood and spider silk
that won't allow you to be break

you were born on a foundation
of glory that will never collapse

John Roedel

no matter how much you shake

I know it feels like you can't go on,
but my love, you simply
must

I know that you have been hurt before,
but my love, it's time to
trust

this is not the end of your story
it's just a welcome sign to
all that you have survived

this is not the finale of your tale
~ it's just the chapter when
you fully come back to life

this wildfire burning around you
in clearing out all that has
already long dead

this screaming that you hear
are just all the ghosts being
evicted from your head

~ welcome to your new life
where the angry ocean
becomes the calm

~ welcome to your what comes next
where all of your swallow scars
become your deepest psalm

~ welcome to your growing power
that you realized once you
left your self-made jail

~ welcome to the adventure
now that you aren't too
terrified to risk and fail

John Roedel

~ welcome to your thumping heart
that has been begging for you
to march along

~welcome to this community of
gathering unafraid burning angels
to which, you belong

~ welcome to your wonderful adventure
don't let anything or anyone
stop your next roll

~welcome to your climb over the mountain
and down into the green valley
of your sweet soul

~welcome to the crossroads
where you refuse to
ever lay down

~ welcome to your royalty
where your bravery is
your glowing crown

John Roedel

#12

I flipped ahead and read the
last few pages of your story
and you need to know something:

everybody that
you have lost
along the way

returns to you
on your last day

~ it turns out that

love is a
boomerang

and it's whistling
through the air
just over the
faraway ridge

~ someday
love is going
to start to bend
it's trajectory
and turn around

and make its way
back to you
just in time
to watch you become
airborne too

you see,
there is no end
to love

there is only

"I'm right here now"

John Roedel

or "I'll be back soon"

our love
for each other
has no straight
edges

our love
for each other
is an easy
curving circle

we are all just
hurtling our
way back
to each other

no matter the
distance

love always
returns

it's a boomerang

and I swear I
can hear it
whistling at us
just beyond
the horizon

John Roedel

#13

Me: Hey God.

God: Hey John.

Me: Grief keeps sneaking up on me.

God: That's because grief is like a ninja.

Me: When will it leave me alone?

God: Hopefully never.

Me: Um. What?!

God: To grieve means that you have loved. Grieving is one of the truest human experiences that you will ever participate in. It often arrives without warning - like a late-day summer storm - obscuring the sun and drenching you in a downpour. It's a gift, isn't it?

Me: Uh, no.

God: Grab a pen and write the following four things down:

1) Grief can come and go as it pleases. You gave it a key to your house at the exact moment you gave your heart to somebody else.

2) Bereavement is the debt you must pay for having loved. There is no getting over the loss of a beloved who is now resting in the arms of endless love. Grief has no expiration date. Despite the passing of time, the phantom pain of mourning is always one memory away from returning.

3) Of all the emotions you face, grief is the by-far stickiest. It gets all over everything. Like peanut butter, grief sticks to the roof of your soul.

4) grief Is like an
afternoon thunderstorm

John Roedel

in late July.

It's the storm
that's always waiting
on the edges
of your most sunny
days to roll
across the horizon
and right over you.

The ghosts of your loved
ones who have died
are the clouds.

The webbed lightning
Illuminating the
dark canvas sky is
their reminder to you
that life is just a
a brilliant temporary flash
of time.

It's the reminder
to live now.
to be bold.
to be electric.

The pounding rain isn't your tears.

It's the hope of eternal life that falls
on you.

It's that downpour of hope that will
help you grow deep roots in love and faith.

The gale winds
of these storms are
the messages from
those you have
lost to death that
are whispering
to you through the pines

John Roedel

the following psalm:

"It's okay, my love. Eternity is holding me. Death isn't an end. Death is a threshold. I'm still here. I never left. Love doesn't die. Love doesn't die. I remain. There is no afterlife. There is only life. I'm here with you. Love doesn't die."

Me: Okay...great...now I'm crying.

God: I'm proud of your tears of grief.

Me: You are?

God: Yes- because it's proof that you have loved.

Me: Well, I've got all sorts of proof pouring down my face right now...

God: It's all such an adventure!!

John Roedel

#14

Recently, I woke up at 4 a.m. feeling crushed under the weight of my anxiety. Unpaid bills. Graying hair. Strained relationships. Health problems of a loved one. Struggling writing career. Relentless bouts of depression. Self-doubt. Anxiety. Regret.

Grief. So much. Grief.

It was all laying on my chest like a cannonball. I have never felt this type of despair before.

I crawled out of my bed and walked across the street to find a park bench to cry alone on. I didn't want my family to see me like this. I didn't want God to see me like this.

I was at the edge of all that I could handle.

I put my hands in my face and just let it all out. Everything I had been holding onto. All my grief. All my sorrow. All of my fear. All of my pain.

It all poured out of my eyes. I hadn't cried like this in a decade. The guttural groaning coming from me probably scared a couple of squirrels into believing a wolf had made its way into town to eat a fat-tailed rodent for a snack.

I cried and cried until the sun came up. With my face buried so deeply in my palms, I could hear my thumping pulse against my cheek. I felt each tear squeeze its way through the gaps in my finger.

It was like I was melting right there on that park bench. I figured in a couple of hours a jogger would have to jump over the middle-aged puddle of clothes and hair that I would soon become.

My inner muse whispered in my ear like she always does in these moments when I'm barely holding on.

She told me to "write something."

John Roedel

That was her usual prescription for helping me through a panic attack like this.

"No," I replied out loud.

The nearby squirrels looked at me with concern in their pebble eyes as I argued with my invisible angels.

I didn't want to put it all on paper -or in this case on my phone. I didn't want to write about this unseen heartbreak I was going through. I didn't want to read it. I just wanted to melt down into a drain. I was too tired to do anything else.

"Open your eyes, John," my muse spoke softly.

"Why?"

"Because you're about to miss it," she said. I swear I could feel a pair of lips kiss my forehead.

I lifted my head. The sun was peeking. The darkness was the one that was melting away and I was still there - yet so was my anxiety.

"Miss what?" I asked.

My muse didn't respond. She didn't have to.

A lovely dragonfly was hovering about four feet away from me. She must have come to the bench to celebrate the coming day. We looked at each other. One of us was breaking and the other was honoring the breaking dawn.

"It's all so beautiful," my muse said through the sound of the dragonfly's whisking wings.

"Yes, it is," I admitted through my post-sob dry heaving.

The dragonfly danced for me. Up, down. Right. Left. It was just the two of us.

"Now...write..." my muse said.

John Roedel

I pulled out my phone and wrote this:

******

I wasn't going to
write a poem today

then I worried that if I didn't
that I might start to forget

how terrifying and beautiful
this whole experience is

I would love to quit writing
about the knots in my stomach
and the rivers of grace I often
find myself swimming naked in

but I think doing they would be
the first step in taking
the mystery of each of those
mystical riddles for granted

and I'd rather be mocked and made
to feel humiliated for my vulnerability

then to be bored

by the distinctive
music that the wings of
a dragonfly makes
when it joins the harmony
of the near-silent sobbing
I produce while sitting at a
park bench at sunup

the frequency of its outstretched wings
the tone of my sentimental tears
blend simultaneously to create
the song of sunrise

John Roedel

two unwitting poets
writing lyrics
together under the
crawling shadows of
first light

one writing with her furious
Anisoptera form

the other with his trembling
hands

both poets unafraid
of remaining authentic
to the growing melody
that's been playing
inside each of them
since they
first hatched

both poets unsure
that they will
survive this day
without being under
the boot of an enemy
we didn't know we had

both poets
recognizing their fragile
role in the beautiful
play they have been
cast in

both poets
equally considered
grotesque or lovely

depending on which
set of eyes look upon
them

both poets taking

John Roedel

inventory and
writing their story

one blurry wing beat
and
one thirsty written line
at a time

a lemonade dragonfly hovering
a blueberry man considering
a pineapple horizon pouring
a pair of cracked coconut wings
a single fresh watermelon smile

a very sweet start
to a very new day

I wasn't going to
write a poem today

but then I remembered
that I was already living

inside of one

John Roedel

#15

Grief is proof
Of love.
Grief is proof
That we have souls.

Grief is proof
That life is
Precious.

I'm glad it hurts
Because it means
That we matter
To one another.

Every tear of
Loss that we shed
Carries with it
The DNA -of the relationship
- Of the love
- Of the story
That two people
Once shared.

Someday I want
My heart to be full of
Potholes and divots.
They will tell the story
Of a heart that was
Willing to be hurt.

Leaving our
Hearts vulnerable
Is an incredible
Act of courage.

I want More of
That kind
Of courage.

Grief is proof

John Roedel

of love.

Grief is proof
of the soul.

Grief is proof
That life is
Precious

#16

these days I'm praying
that God

gives me the courage to
remember that I'm a just
tourist in this world

and when the
moment comes
when I have to
board the train
to return from
wherever it is that
I came from

help me to remember that I don't
get to take anything with me

customs gets it all

I'm not allowed to smuggle any
souvenirs with me that I've
accumulated while I was on Earth

everything
must go into the bins

life is like one of those all-inclusive resorts
that doesn't let me take anything with me
when it's time for me to go

when I'm following the cosmic
train whistle to make my way
back to eternity

I have to let it all go

nothing comes with me

John Roedel

~ no postcards from all the little villages I stayed in while I was here that I meant to send to you

~ no cute magnets with pithy little pearls of wisdom about hope or cats that I bought from a rickety souvenir stand

~ no gold coins with ghostly presidents on their faded faces

~ no books that I pretended I was reading on the beach whenever you walked by

~ no maps that never kept me from getting lost in the woods

~ no grudges that I've kept fresh in my hotel ice bucket

~ no regrets that I watched in the movie theatre of my mind every night

~ no commemorative t-shirts about the time I won a Twitter fight

I will leave it all behind

nothing I'm clinging to in my hands
gets to come with me

because

the place where I'm returning to
has no need for such things

~ when the conductor shouts
"All aboard!"

and my vacation here on Earth
comes to an end

I will drop everything and
leave it all behind

everything

except for my

John Roedel

Upon Departure 68

thoughts of you

~ they are coming with me

I'll hide my memories of you
in the back pockets of my soul
and only let them out once I cross
the border that exists between
temporary dust and everlasting spirit

I'll hold the last kiss you will give me
under my tongue until the coast is
clear and I can open my mouth
to let it out

and watch as our shared
romance turns into a
bright blue butterfly

my love,

the closer I get to the end of
my vacation

the less I want to take back home
with me

~ I only want to bring
your scent and the countless
sweet sentiments you wove into
the tapestry of my memory

even though I'll be a spirit
  you will be the one haunting me

oh, my love,

~and when your vacation
comes to an end

~and you have to
follow the whistle

John Roedel

~and you have to
unclench your hands
and let everything go

~and you have to board
the train to the next place

don't fret
I'll meet you when
you get there

I'll be counting the moments
until I get to see you
walk off the train car and onto
the marble platform

you'll find me once you
look past the rolling steam
and the ribbons of glowing stardust

you'll see me
standing right
on the platform

I'll be the one covered in
bright blue butterflies
and holding up a sign that reads

"I never forgot you."

John Roedel

#17

forgive like a comet
is about to hit

hug like the hourglass
is about empty

sing like your voice
is about to go mute

kiss like the candle
is about to burn out

howl like the moon
is about to be stolen

dance like the ground
is about to break open

write like the ink is
about to run dry

treat others today like they
are about to be gone tomorrow

pray like the world
is about on its final spin

laugh like your tears
are about to return

give like Heaven
is about to audit you

watch a sunrise like
you're about to go blind

hold someone like
you're about to become a ghost

~ it's all about time

John Roedel

be desperate to
   live and to
love a little bit recklessly

caution is a luxury
for those who have
endless days to be patient

~ we don't

everything is temporary

   the calendar is flipping
so fast that it's become
a wind tunnel

it's all about time

~ that's what makes
it is such an adventure

fall into this sacred moment
~ it's really all we have

spend every second
as if you are stargazing
from a hospice bed

fall into this sacred
moment with me

no more unspoken words
no more unmentioned mercies
no more unthawed hearts
no more unforgivable sins
no more unopened eyes
no more unfelt tendernesses
no more unlit candles
no more unkind comments
no more unattended gardens
no more unfinished poems

John Roedel

Upon Departure 72

no more unheard pardons
no more unremarkable kisses
no more unbelieved compliments
no more unaware ignorance
no more unappreciated miracles
no more unopened doors
no more unhealthy relationships
no more unrecorded songs
no more unclimbed mountains
no more understated sentiments
no more unwritten love letters
no more unfollowed dreams
no more unheralded angels
no more unrealized opportunities
no more untouched conversations
no more unthought wishes
no more unuttered prayers
no more untrue sermons
no more unneeded desires
no more unnecessary worry
no more unused dancing shoes
no more unlocked vaults
no more unthoughtful insults
no more untied knots
no more unhappy compromises
no more unread psalms
no more unsealed tombs
no more untaken journeys
no more unseen wonderment

~ no more

these seconds
are racing by

let's not waste
any more of them

sit with me now
and wrap your
legs between mine

John Roedel

and let's laugh
together wildly
under this beautiful
falling sky

fall into this sacred
moment with me

it's really all we have

it's all about time

John Roedel

#18

my love,

don't let your
skin become
so thick that
nothing can
hurt you anymore

getting wounded
is part of the experience

the scars you
collect are all
part of your story

take off your armor
and give vulnerability
a chance to paint
your naked form

feel the sunlight
on your shoulders

let the wind move
through your hair

give your tears a
chance to be counted

allow us to be swept
up in your smile

you see, my love,

you weren't born
to be hidden behind
a towering wall

you were formed out
of an ancient whisper to

John Roedel

become a natural wonder
where we all gather to
listen to the songbirds
sing through the pines of
your evergreen beauty

you were given this skin
to be kissed softly
- don't let it grow scales

you were given your eyes
to reflect starlight
- don't close them to keep us from
seeing your soul

you were given your hands
to lace inside another hand
- don't keep them constantly
folded in your lap

my love,

I know this world
can be a sharpened spear
that will often pierce you

but

when given a choice
bleeding is always
better than apathy

someday when we
meet in the moving
cosmic river that exists
on the crawling fringe
of everything

let's take turns
washing each other's
scars while saying
the same prayer

John Roedel

over and over

"I got this wound
for caring and I
got this one for
having an open heart

but that is the cost
that comes from being
a work of sacred art."

John Roedel

#19

I've learned to
turn my grief
I feel for you
into a kiss that I blow
into the breeze
every morning

A floating kiss
that can be carried by
trade winds and
jet streams and
cosmic flows

over alien mountains
around swirling nebulas
through thin wormholes
and under the edge of the universe

to find you
wherever you are

and to land
right on your
glowing cheek

and to remind you
that there is no
distance too great
for us

when you feel
my windblown kiss
on your face

you'll know

that the candle
we lit together
long ago still burns

John Roedel

Upon Departure 78

our love is a flame
and we are the wick

and we are endless

my love,
I'm kissing the air
again right now

and I know you
can still feel it

and I know you
can still feel me

and I know this
is just the beginning
of our story

John Roedel

#20

this isn't going to be one of
those inspirational poems

that tells you that everything
is always to be okay

because sometimes it won't
and sometimes you won't be ok either

what in the hell does
being ok mean anyway?

does being ok mean that we can muster the strength to fake
smile our way through the day until we get home where the
shadows are ready to convert us to their dark theology?

does being ok mean that we can go an hour without feeling like
our skin is trying to crawl right off of our body?

does being ok mean that we avoid looking at ourselves in a mirror
because our reflection looks like a stranger?

is any of that ok?

this isn't going to be one of
those inspirational poems

that is going to act as if peace
is just one sunrise away

because there will be a time when
mercy is late because it missed the bus

there will be a night night
that feels so terribly endless

and someday your life will feel
like hope exists for everybody else but you

this isn't going to be one of

John Roedel

those inspirational poems

that tells you that there will always be somebody there to pick you up when you fall down

because there
won't always be

there will be a day when you
will feel abandoned by everybody

there will be a day when the reason you are on the ground is
 because somebody put you there

there will be a day when somebody you love tells you that they wish you were never born and for a brief moment you will start to wish for the same thing

this poem isn't about how to make your life
look like the perfectly crafted
Instagram feed of your
old friend from high school
who apparently never has a bad day

you know who I am talking about

> this isn't a poem about being "Amaze-balls"
> or about "Living Your Best Life"
> or about making lemonade out of lemons
> or about chasing rainbows
> or about always being in love with yourself
> or about how your suffering has a purpose
> or about letting go of the past
> or listening to your inner child

~ those would make really great poems

but that isn't what
this poem about

THIS is a poem
about the exact moment when you are

John Roedel

shattered on the bathroom floor
holding on to your life by a couple
of the remaining threads you have
to your happiest of childhood memories
while feeling like there is an invisible
monster chewing straight through
the center of your heart

THIS is a poem
for that moment
when grief is pressing
it's hands up against your
mouth and you can't hear
anything else but the
sound of your own
muffled screaming

THIS is a poem
for that exact moment
when despair crams its tongue
into your ear and whispers
the most unholy lies about you

THIS is a poem
for that exact moment
when you don't think you
can hold on for one more
second because you
have become your
own atheist

my love,

THIS is a poem
that was written to
remind you that
are more powerful
than any supernova
that has ever lit up
a dark vacuum

you were born

John Roedel

Upon Departure 82

out of the same
energy that formed the sun

*your heart is still covered
in first day stardust*

you've just forgotten
about the power that sits
dormant inside of you

you are the
Yellowstone Caldera
that has grown pregnant
with the rock molten lava of purpose
and a blinding light of fury that can be seen
by the angels vacationing on Alpha Centauri

you are just about ready
to explode
and to terraform this world

it's all about to happen

the thing is,
you've just forgotten about the
fire inside of you

if you close your eyes
and hold your breath
for the briefest of moments
you will feel the glow
from the embers
laying deep
inside of you

go ahead and do it
I'll wait

close your eyes
hold your breath

John Roedel

hold on
hold on
now exhale

there it is
can you see the thin blue flame?
can you feel the growing heat?

the fire in you is still there

it's ready
for you to explode

warm your hands
by your dreams
for a bit before
you go and remake
this world with your
steel-melting gaze

~the fire in you might be faint right now
~the fire in you might be barely flickering

but it's there

it's just buried under the layers and layers
of your scar tissue

it's a fire that isn't going anywhere

okay, my love,
I'm going to be honest,
the fire isn't simply inside of you

I just said that to get your attention

the thing is,
you aren't separate from this fire

you aren't two different
compounds being mixed together
by a mortar and pestle

John Roedel

Upon Departure 84

you are the fire

yes, even when your life
is not ok

you are still the fire

even when you
aren't ok

you are still the fire

and you will survive
and you will burn like a candle of revelation

yes, even when the
dawn takes the day off

you are the fire

you can become
your own sunrise

you can become
your own sunrise

THIS is a poem
about learning
that you are not
your pain

that isn't who you are

~also while we are at:

you are not your heartbreaks
you are not your failures
you are not your tears
you are not your scars

those things aren't who you are

John Roedel

what you are is much
more ancient and eternal

*you are the fire
even when you are broken*

you are rolling magma
even when you feel cold as winter

you are the supernova
even when you are spilled out on the floor
like an open bottle of pills
that you are tempted to swallow all at once

you are the fire

that's what THIS poem is about

it's about you
my furious crimson flame

and I can't wait to see how
you set this world ablaze

John Roedel

#21

I'm still eight-years-old

and I'm riding my bike
over dirt hills
while being chased
by neighborhood bullies

I'm still eighty-eight
and I'm riding in an ambulance
over to the hospice
and preparing to turn my
bruised skin in for pastel
colored orbs of light

I'm still eighteen
and riding the
rollercoaster of
my racing heart
as I feel her lips
melt against mine like
summer cotton candy

I'm still sixty-eight
and I'm riding on a thin boat
across a fat lake and
laughing as the cold
waves splash my face

I'm still twenty-eight
and I'm riding a lumbering
brown horse through
a trail in the purple rocky mountains
and listening to angels sing
to me through the pines
and for the very first time
in a long time,
I believe in the
unseen again

I'm still fifty-eight

John Roedel

and I'm riding an elevator up
to the top floor to try and convince
a room full of people in pantsuits
to believe in poetry

I'm still thirty-eight
and I'm riding my anger
as I stumble into a church
and scream up into the
rafters for God to talk to me

I'm still forty-eight
and I'm riding an airplane
to meet God for coffee
under a tree in faraway
New Zealand

it's still all happening at once

I'm still riding all of these memories
at the same time

bikes, ambulances, heartbeats,
boats, horses, elevators, teardrops
and airplanes

everything in my life
has been a vehicle

carrying me from one moment to the next

 ~ but it isn't happening to
me in chronological order

I'm still a child

and I'm still a fading hospice patient
and I'm still a wide-eyes romantic
and I'm still a giggling wave runner
and I'm still a wanna-be cowboy
and I'm still a struggling poet
and I'm still a cautious blasphemer

John Roedel

Upon Departure 88

and I'm still a spiritual explorer

I'm still all of that right now
   -even the moments that haven't occurred

- especially those

- I can feel the gravity of the
future pulling on my bones

- to a place that I know I have been before

because many of my favorite
memories of my life are
the ones that the calendar says
haven't happened yet

yet I know they have

~ it's all happening at once to me

my past, present and future
and swimming in the same
pool of tears that I leave on
my breakfast table every morning

it's all such an adventure

John Roedel

#22

the moon was taking
questions this morning

so I asked her

"What is grief?"

and she said

"Grief is a stretching field full
of thick beautiful rose bushes
and bees that you must travel
through to get to the other side

and each rose is a memory
of the person you lost

and every time you
smell a memory rose
you get stung by a bee

and get your face
scratched by the
sharp thorns

and by the time you
reach the end of the
field you are covered
in wounds."

I sat down on the curb
and thought for a moment

so I asked

"Okay, but once I
get through the field
of grief what is waiting
for me on the other side
of it?"

John Roedel

the moon replied:

"On the other side of the field of
grief is another- even bigger field
of grief that has even more beautiful
rose bushes and even angrier bees
and even more pointy thorns that you
must get through."

"Come to think of it, the moon continued.
"On the other side of that field
of grief is another field
and then another and other,

in fact, I don't think the fields
ever actually end

they just get bigger,

the fields of roses, thorns and bees
cover every horizon

with each field becoming more
lovely and painful than the last."

my heart sank

"Why would I want to
travel through that field
if there is no end to it?

Why would I want to
move through grief
if there is no other side
to it?"

the moon's reflection
turned a shade of blue
and said

"So you can remember your loved one

John Roedel

who has departed."

my bottom lip trembled as I asked

"But there will be so many thorns and bees."

she smiled and replied

"And it will hurt

but you simply have
to smell these roses;

they smell just like
yesterday."

then the moon fell asleep
behind a cloud

and I stayed awake

plotting my course through
the lush thorny field
of buzzing rose bushes
and aching memories
spilled out in front of me

John Roedel

#24

"It's Hard To Hold Hands With a Fist"

"I hate. I hate. I hate," my mom chanted unconsciously on her deathbed.

"It's going to be okay. Everything is going to be okay," I lied softly to her while holding her cold, clenched fist in my hand.

With her eyes pinched shut she responded with another round of, "I hate. I hate. I hate."

It had been five days since she had said anything other than "I hate" and it was breaking my heart. The "I hates" always came in threes. I spent hours by her bedside trying to figure out why. I had considered for a while that she was trying to communicate with me through some sort of metaphysical code. Perhaps she was telling me to make sure to water her plants three times a day? I made a couple of dozen "I hate" anagrams trying to solve the mystery.

Eat Hi – A referendum against the art of small talk that we both despised with every particle in our bodies.

Ha Tie – A joke between us because I never tied my shoes and she was certain that someday I'd trip in a super embarrassing situation? (note: I still don't tie my shoes to this day and I'm awaiting her ghostly "Told you so." that will most likely follow once I go barreling down the stands during my son's upcoming high school graduation.

The IA – Did she want me to take her to Iowa? Was this like Field of Dreams? I've always fancied myself as a lower rent version of Kevin Costner - provided he had a medical condition that caused him to shrink about a foot and lose some of his trademarked smolder.

Eventually, it became clear that there was no hidden message in what she was saying. The endless stream of socially awkward neurologists made it known to us that whatever my mom was saying was probably just her brain misfiring due to the trauma of the collecting pressure of blood that was building on it.

"I hate. I hate. I hate."

I didn't want those to be the last words that she would utter before the unstoppable bleeding in her brain would finally claim her life. I was desperate for her to say anything else.

"It is going to be okay. You are loved. You are looooovveed. Loooved." I said, like a parent trying to get their baby to say their first word.

Although I am prone to abject selfishness and can easily make most things become about me, I was pretty sure that her litany of I hates didn't have much to do with how she felt about me. Although we definitely had a perfect strangers kind of relationship we weren't estranged. If I had to guess, I'm pretty sure she was just commenting on how much she really disliked her current situation. My mom abhorred doctors and people fussing over her and here she was enduring both horrors at once.

I remember trying to hold her hand, but it was always clenched too tight, so I settled for just resting mine on top of hers while watching her fade away.

I sat by her for another three days in that grim little hospital room, witnessing her grapple with death. I imagined during that time that they were tied up in some pretty heated negotiations.

Death: Alright, let's go.
My Mom: Shut up.
Death: Please?
My Mom: Bite me.
Death: I'll go make some coffee.
My Mom: Make a double pot. You're gonna be here a while.
Death: Great...

Eventually, my mom was moved to a much more comfortable hospice center for her last couple of days on Earth. There were no more mechanical whirls or beeps from monitors that plagued our days together in the old hospital room. At the hospice center, there was only the sound of quiet dignity of my mom's final few thousand breaths. It was so much more relaxed and reverent there. But there was one familiar sound that followed us to the hospice:

"I hate. I hate. I hate," she continued.

"It's going to be okay," I responded on cue. My hand around her fist.

A young hospice nurse walked in and took a look at the two of us. We were quite a pair. My mom fading away and me looking like I hadn't showered since the late 90s.

"Hold her hand," the nurse instructed kindly but firmly. That's a difficult balance in tone to manage, but she did it.

I tried to explain that my mom wasn't going to allow for that. Her hand was too tightly coiled. The nurse shook her head like a fastball pitcher who had just been given the sign to throw a changeup. She walked over and took my mom's fisted hand, gently turned it over and began to tenderly massage the base of her palm. Within a second or two her fist opened up like a spring flower and I was able to lace my fingers with hers.

This was the first time we had held hands in over 25 years. My hand and hers were slowly sewn together by the angels who frequent hospice rooms. We weren't just two humans saying goodbye. We were a mother and a son saying every unspoken word that remained between us through the warmth of hands being cradled by one another.

Everything melted away. The room. The lovely hospice nurse. It was just my mom and me. A mother and her son having one last walk together through the universe. Two souls parting. Saying everything that needed to be said.

When I regained my senses I saw the nurse on the other side of my mom's bed holding her opposite hand.

She smiled at me:

John Roedel

"It's hard to hold hands with a fist," the nurse said in the softest of voices.

I nodded in agreement. I was crying. It was the first time that I had broken down during my mom's six-week battle.

"It's going to be okay. You are loved," I whispered to my mom.

"Okay…" she whispered in reply.

She never spoke again.

A day later my mom passed away surrounded by family and with her hands being held. She ventured across the veil and into God's arms while feeling a pulse beat against her still body.

"Okay" was her last word.

Perfect.

Every day I
Try my
Best to
Remember the
Final lesson
My mom
Taught me:
Live with
Open hands
And not
Clenched fists.
Okay.
I will.
I will.
Okay.

John Roedel

#24

people will deny
anything these days

so, I have decided to join
the practice of dismissing things
that we've been told are true

I have decided to quit believing in death

~ it just doesn't exist
for me anymore

instead,

I have a new theory
    I'm working on:

when our dear ones
depart their bodies and
turn back into air and light

they don't disappear
behind a brick wall
that separates us

~there are no bricks
there is no wall
   ~there are no barriers

there is only a grand
window between us
and those whom we
have stitched ourselves
to with the most divine
of angel hair threads

we can see our beloveds in
the heart shape clouds
and they can see us
as we kiss their picture

John Roedel

goodnight ever so softly

death doesn't exist
it's a debunked
flat-earth theology

where we are told that
the people we love spill off the
edge of the world and
fall away from us into
the endless unknown

that's not my experience

what I have seen is that when
a dear one leaves me I don't
feel the space grow between us

I feel us grow closer together
   ~ our entanglement becomes tighter

they travel with me to the
store to buy garlic

they brush my hair out of my eyes while
I cry in my car in an empty parking lot

they join me on my daily
walk around a lake

they sit on the board of my conscious
and offer me advice

they float above me while
I write a poem

they laugh when I trip over the same
chair damn every day

they catch my prayers and
courier them to God

John Roedel

they write love notes to me with steam
on my bathroom mirror

they play the right songs on the radio
at just the right time

they have made a cottage
in my heart
they have turned my eyes
into miracle telescopes

they converted my lungs
into a retreat center

they dance in the eyes
of my children

my loved ones haven't gone anywhere
and neither have yours

they are just on the other side of the window

waiting for you to see them
waving at you
in their sundresses made out of stars
and their tuxedos stitched by time

and someday I will be on the
other side of the glass

acting so obnoxious that you
won't be able to ignore me

and someday I will be writing
you love notes on the petals
of sunflowers for you to find
just when you need to read them

and someday I will help paint a
sunset in the exact color of the
way I felt whenever I was wrapped
up tightly in your arms

John Roedel

I'm no scientist but
my research tells me that
death doesn't exist

however, love does
and it has no end

and neither do we

John Roedel

#25

where I'm from,

we have angels
who slip across from
the beyond every
midnight in February
just to write their
love letters for us on
our trees with the
tiniest of frozen pencils

can't you see it, my love?

the devil isn't in the
details

the divine is

in the frost
there is a drop
of holy water holding
it's breath for
spring so it can
feed the roses

I'm holding my
breath too

because I believe
that

everything frozen
will someday melt

the anticipation of
spring is what makes
the colors of April baptize
us in the pastel swirl of
resurrection

John Roedel

without the grey
how would we
have ever come to
fall in love with the green?

these frozen,
suspended love letters
from the angels in
the trees are telling us

to hold on

the nights are getting shorter
~ the daylight is starting to win

hold on

everything that freezes
will melt

all that is captured
by death
shall be set free

even me
even me
even me

oh, God,
let it
even be me

John Roedel

#26

I've spent half my life
counting the change in
my pockets to make sure
that I can pay the fare for
the bus ride to heaven

turns out the bus
was never coming

I wasted so much time

I should have noticed that I've been
the only one sitting here waiting
in this abandoned bus stop

but I was so busy looking at
the map on my phone trying
to figure out what connections
I needed to make on my route
to Heaven that I didn't see the
cobwebs growing on my heart

so yesterday I left the
bus stop to Heaven

and now I'm spending my time
at a little lake just behind the
the bus stop where all the
fat robins gather in the
trees to sing about
the promise of eternal spring

it's a little spot
where the wild grass
pokes up between
bare toes and
the air smells like raw honey

and everyone who
has ever held my hand

John Roedel

before is here wearing their
sundresses and corduroys

and they're so happy
that I finally made it

and now I understand why
there was never any
bus in the first place

John Roedel

#27

So it's the end of your life
and you're thinking about all
that you've done

Did you only chase money?
Did you have any fun?

Did you spend any time
in wonderment staring up
at the sky?

Or just you just look at your phone
as time slipped on by?

It's the end of your life
and your remembering
all that you've seen

Did you only look into mirrors?
Did you memorize your dreams?

Did you get to witness one
true miracle while you
hurried about

Or did you trade all your unseen faith in
for a lifetime of tangible doubt?

It's the end of your life
and your asking
what was its point

Was it to serve or to hoard?
Was it to curse or to anoint?

Did you ever stand in moving
water and feel the great
mystic flow?

Or were you so afraid of drowning

John Roedel

Upon Departure 105

that the shore is all you know

It's the end of your life
and you're reflecting on
all the people you met

Did you forgive them for wounding you?
Did you add interest to their debts?

Did you hold on tightly to your
grudges like they were the last
gold coins you own

Or did leave them behind you because
of how heavy they'd grown?

It's the end of your life
and you're considering how
you aided the poor

Did you live with open hands?
Did you make your heart a closed door?

Did you become an ambassador
to charity by giving more
then you take?

Did you only help others when cameras were watching
or was your generosity fake?

It's the end of your life
and you're worried about
the words that you used

Did you offer psalms of blessings?
Did you speak to only abuse?

Did you do your best to say
all the things that can't remain
unsaid?

Or did you not say "I love you"

John Roedel

enough before you were dead?

When you're on your last
breath - I hope you don't
hopelessly wonder

why for so long did you wait

to live with fierce
kindness and passion?

because then - it'll be too late

John Roedel

#28

Me: Hey God.

God: Hey John.

Me: When will I ever get over grieving the death of someone that I love?

God: Never. Grief doesn't end. It doesn't come and go like a summer storm. It's in the air around you. Grief is permanent. That feeling of loss doesn't have a deadline - it's a wound that becomes the aching scar. After somebody that you love dies it feels as if you have lost a limb. Even years later there can be phantom pains that can send you to your knees. As long as you are alive on Earth, grief will be with you in one form or another.

Me: That's terrible. I'd like to move on. It's been years.

God: There is no moving on. There is no "getting over" the death of a beloved. Why would you want to?

Me: So that I can stop having these unexpected pangs of sadness hit me out of the blue.

God: That's actually a wonderful thing. It means that you have loved somebody so much that their absence in your life is still so felt deeply. There is no more profound human experience than to grieve. It means that you have given a piece if your heart to someone else.

Me: But when that person passes away that piece goes with them.

God: That's the debt you must pay for taking the risk to love somebody else. You are sending your heart to heaven one little bit at a time. You are joining eternity through piecemeal. That part of your love for them has moved on with that person when they die - but it's not gone forever! When you join those that you have lost in the great beyond someday you get back and all the pieces that went ahead of you. Eventually, your heart will be whole again. I promise.

John Roedel

Me: It's so hard when I can have an unexpected sudden wave of emotion pass over me. It can be triggered by something so little. A particular scent, a song on the radio, or a random memory popping up in my head. I have no warning when I am overcome with grief.

God: That is the way grief works. Like I told you - grief never leaves you. As long as you keep the memory of your loved one in your heart that grief will be always lurking. I'm glad that you used the word "wave" earlier. That is exactly how grief can work. Grief is a tide. Somedays the tide is high. Somedays the tide is low. Either way, it's always there on your shore.

Me: If that's true - how do you expect me to function?

God: Because you owe it to the ones that you have lost to live life to its fullest. You can honor their lives by living yours with wild abandon. If you were to die today you wouldn't want those who love you to give up and quit, right? You would want your survivors to keep on keeping on, right? Grief doesn't always mean being sad. Grief can arrive equally in laughter and anger - it is more than just a single emotional response. To lament the loss of someone means celebrating their life by cherishing and clinging to those memories with them like prized treasures. Grief doesn't require you to cry. The only requirement that grief has for you is to not close the door on your love for those who have passed away. Keep their memory alive.

Me: This would all be easier for us to understand if you didn't allow death in the first place. You put amazing people in my life and then You take them away. Just like that, they are gone.

God: Just because your beloved has died, it doesn't mean that they are gone. They are waiting for you across the veil. Love doesn't go away when the body fails. Love is everlasting. Shared love is immortal. Your grief is a temple in your heart that honors that love. The way of life is to love and be loved so deeply that someday people will profoundly grieve your passing.

Me: Death is so scary. I'm terrified of the end.

John Roedel

God: John Boy - death is just the beginning.

Me: Of what?

God: Your adventures.

John Roedel

#29

Dear, you,

*Grief is a tear
that keeps freezing
and unfreezing on
your cheek*

It's okay.

*It's supposed to be
like that.*

*Having persistently red cheeks
Is how grief is designed to look like*

*Love,
me*

#30

Is it your turn to forgive me
or
is it my turn to forgive you?

I can't remember either.

To be safe we better just forgive
each other at the exact same time.

Here's how:

We will hold hands
so that your wrist
presses against mine.

And now we wait
until our pulses
match each other.

And now we close our
eyes and pretend
that our veins are
rivers of empathy

and now the seasons are changing

and now the mountains are melting

and now the water is rising

and now the rivers are growing together

and now the barren
space we let grow
between us is being
flooded with stretching
vineyards of clemency

and now exotic wildflowers
are growing everywhere

John Roedel

Upon Departure 112

everywhere
everywhere
everywhere

and now all we know is an ocean

and now we are swimming
in the same tides of understanding

and now the two of us are endless again

and now we are the
newborn children of forgiveness

open your eyes
look down at our wrists
wrapped around each other

and now I forgive you
and now you forgive me

and now I see you
and now you see me

and now can't you feel it?

this rising river
this rolling ocean
this endless us

this rushing mercy

John Roedel

#31

What you are lying on is
more than a simple bed
It's more than just for sleep
Or a place to lay your head

It's a cocoon made of healing
It's a cradle made for rest
It's a garden of comfort
It's a chapel most blessed

This bed is also an easy river
That it will carry you gently along
As your body finds quiet respite
While the angels paint the dawn

May this bed bless you with renewal
May your fears - it help release
May this bed wrap you in recovery
May it provide you with peace

What you are laying on
is more than a simple bed
It's a soft cloud of remedy
With serenity in its threads

So take all the time you need
To find the strength inside of you
May your dreams be full of light
As your life is remade anew

John Roedel

#32

Something is happening inside of me. I'm changing. I'm starting to see things that other people don't. I'm starting to feel invisible hands holding me upright. I'm starting to constantly hear a choir singing from behind the moon at night. I'm starting to taste on my tongue every single time I breathe. I'm starting to levitate whenever you aren't looking at me. I'm starting to be able to break clouds apart by just staring at them.

Oh, okay, now that I say all of that out loud I can understand why you are looking at me that way. Maybe I'm off the map a little. Maybe this shift in me is all in my mind. Maybe. Probably not. But maybe.

please
can you just give me
a chance to explain it
to you again?

I found a
phone on
the side of
a tree in
the park
by my house
where I
can call my dad
in heaven.

It only appears
one day
a year
- usually in September.

The phone
smells like
pine and
my fathers
favorite old
golf shirts.

John Roedel

There is
no keypad
or rotary dial
to this phone
and there is no
mouthpiece.

There is
only a cup
for my ear
to listen in
and a wire made
out of dark vines
that disappear into the
bark.

When I
touch the
cold smooth
chestnut receiver
to my ear
the tree
begins to
oscillate.

Like an idling
lawnmower.

Soon I
am shaking
right along with it.

The birds
go quiet.

The normally
outspoken Wyoming
wind hushes.

Everything is so still.

So so so so

John Roedel

still

The only thing
I can hear is the
soft hum from
the dial tone that
only exists in
the phones connect
our world to the
after place.

I've tried explaining
to a priest what
this dial tone sounds like
but I can't find the right words
that doesn't make me seem
like I should be medicated.

It sounds like the
color of pink?

Does that help? No?

Okay, how about this:

Can you imagine
what a river would
sound like if it could
sing you a song
while you stood in the middle of it?

It's like that but
joined by the sound of
a hundred
million butterflies
beating their wings
all around you.

It's the ancient melody
that only the instruments
of flow and wings

John Roedel

can produce.

It's both the tone of
grateful river water
and the thunder
of countless dancing
spotted kaleidoscopes
all playing their music
in harmony.

I know that doesn't make any sense
but that is exactly how it sounds.
Don't look at me that way.
I'm not crazy.
I know how this sounds

Then I hear his voice -
the voice of my father who
has been gone over twenty years.

"My son," my dad says softly in my ear.

I can hear children laughing in the background.
I can hear what sounds like a big marching band playing behind him.
Despite the noise, his voice cuts through everything

and then always
says the same thing:

"Love never dies."

After that, he hangs up
and the phone that
I'm holding turns
to bark

and I turn into melting wax
under the final hot breaths that
come from a failing September sky.

I sit by the tree

John Roedel

Upon Departure 118

        covered in
        sap and leaves
        and memory

    Usually, I will remain
    and cry for an hour

      but not because
      I'm sad

       but because I
       know that all
       of the connections
       we make here on Earth
       are everlasting.

   They go on and on and on
   and whenever I think about that

      I can't stop crying.

        I pull myself
        up by the tree
        and dry my eyes
        with my sleeves.

Don't look at me like that.

I know what you're thinking.
I'm not crazy.
Let me explain...

I know that we have a difference
of opinion when it comes to loss.

Some believe grief is meant to bury us.
While you and I believe grief lifts us up.

The work of grief isn't
to destroy us

it's to get us to

           John Roedel

pay attention to
the miracle of now.

Nothing is promised.
Not tomorrow.
Not even our next breath.

Grief is here to tell us
to keep our eyes open
right now
because they might not
be tomorrow.

I rise from my grief
because I know
that it is the cost
of loving somebody else
with every particle of
my curvy little being.

Grief is the bill
that our heart owes
when our beloved leaves us

but

Grief is not
my enemy.

Grief is my
life coach.

Constantly reminding
me that our skin
is temporary but
the relationships we
make are eternal.

I rise from my grief so
I can make it
to my next
September phone call

John Roedel

with my dad.

Don't look at me like that.
Listen to me,
please.

I rise from my
grief because

love never
dies.

Love never dies. Love never dies. Love never dies.

John Roedel

#33

grief made me a garden
and allowed the dandelions
to wildly grow

grief laid me in weeds
and kindly told me to wait
for the wind to blow

with every new gale
came a parade of
bright blowing seeds

with every fall gust
I could feel a little
more of my hurt finally leave

out in the air
went the pieces
of my poor fractured heart

out in the sky
I watched my pain
turn into untethered art

grief isn't meant
for us to clutch up,
hoard or to tightly hold

grief is the way
that the story of
of loved ones can be told

to share their path
and their spirit
and their lives

is exactly how
grief allows their
memory to survive

John Roedel

grief is a garden
full of things
that we thought were dead

but death isn't
final because it's
only our skin that we shed

so lay me down softly
in a thousand yellow dandelions
and all around me, they will grow

until the forever wind comes
to tell the story of my life
when it's finally my time to go

John Roedel

#34

it appears that I fell out of my body
-and right up into the light
and no, it doesn't really bother me
-that I've lost all of my sight

because now I can see with
-the wide eyes of my heart
and I can no longer tell
-my friends or foes apart

currently, I'm out deep in space
-watching the birth of a baby star
yet despite our physical separation
-from you, my soul's never that far

tomorrow, I'll be picking flowers
-in the garden out near the edge of time
I can send you a rose by angel mail
-if of my survival, you need a fragrant sign

my love, I know you'll come to find me
-once you'll fall up into the light, too
and we'll slow dance by disco nebulas
-and kiss until purple comets blush blue

our reunion will be an interstellar romantic ritual
-out here among the burst of creation's first light
where the two of us will become an Andromeda knot
-that is tied together so softly -yet tangled so tight

and when our souls become one
-we'll open up our own little cosmic shop
we'll call our boutique "Death Isn't Real"
-since the love between us never stopped

tethered as one we will spend ten billion years
-until the bolts of eternity start to unscrew
yet I won't fear the great resetting of time
-because it means I'll get to discover you anew

John Roedel

so, my love, when forever starts all over
~we'll both fall back into our new skin
and we'll find each other on an alien shore
~to let our love story start all over again

John Roedel

#35

when somebody else tries
to tell you how you should grieve

smile and forgive them
through your watering eyes

and then imagine
how lonely it must be
to be the person who
audits the tears
of other people

the well-intended
will tell you how
long you should miss
your beloved

but

you take your time

grief is a hedge maze
and being lost inside of it

is more than okay

don't race through
your heartache

because you might
just miss a miracle
or two

in the teardrops rolling
down your face

don't grieve quickly
just to make somebody
else feel better

John Roedel

Upon Departure 126

if you need to,
let your grief
become a coral reef

let the algae of your hurt
slowly form over the years
into the softest violet hue of heaven

it can take two lifetimes to recover

when our beloved becomes
an empty chair

it's okay

take as much time
as you need

your healing is your healing

and the scars of absence
will itch longer than you can imagine

but that is because you
risked to love so deeply

and that is far better than
the alternative

I am proud of you

and the courage it
takes for you to grieve
so fearlessly

don't listen to those
who want you to go back
to normal

normal will never exist again
for those of us who have
lost a part of our heart

John Roedel

if the moon broke in half
would it feel normal?

to hell with normal

> *normal* was their scent on your collar
> *normal* was their voice resting in your ear
> *normal* was their touch on your skin

you have a new normal

it's looking at the shape of clouds
for messages from the great beyond
that your beloved is fine

you have a new normal

it's building a cabin in
the woods of your memory
where you and your beloved
can meet for lunch

you have a new normal

it's crying and laughing
at the same time
whenever their favorite
song plays on the radio

grief isn't the enemy
of life

numbness is

don't become numb to your suffering

welcome it in
and let it wrap you
up like a blanket

whenever it shows up

John Roedel

at your door

it's okay

I swear

it's okay

your beloved misses you just
as much as you miss them

and someday
you two will
get all tangled up
together again

someday
you two will
push each on a
swing again under
a shower of falling blooms

and someday
you two will ride
comets together
on the edge of everything

and someday
you two will giggle
at all of the people
who tried to tell you

how to grieve

John Roedel

#36

hope is often
so much quieter
than fear

hope is the whisper
between screams

hope is the muted hum
of the world moving under your feet

hope is the sleepy song
being sung to us in the midst
of the fury of exploding bombs

hope is the nearly inaudible
sound of your tears drying
on the rose of your cheek

hope is the hushed wind passing
through a tall Wyoming pine

hope is the noise of you
softly exhaling while
looking for God in the mirror

hope is the sound of stars winking
at us from across the cosmos

~ hope is the babbling river
~ hope is the snoring baby
~ hope is the thumping heartbeat

hope is a lightly
beeping hospital monitor

hope is the sound
of butterfly wings
moving in the spring

hope is the noise ice

John Roedel

makes as it melts on a lake

hope is the gentle scratching of
a flower as it claws its way
out of the earth to sunbathe

hope is never loud
   hope is never fussy
hope is never announced
- in fact, you might miss hope's
arrival if you're not listening for it

hope is more piano
then it is a saxophone

~ hope is humble
~ hope is stealthy
~ hope doesn't wear a name tag

hope is so often so silent

but that what
makes hope so
powerful

because it can
surprise us at a moment's notice

hope is always present
 it's the beat between music notes

it's the lips smack before the kiss
   it's a deep breath before the eulogy

hope is the quiet voice of God
that is endlessly begging us to
not surrender to the crawling shadows

and the voice is always
saying the same thing:

"Hold on, my love, hold on, my love."

John Roedel

if you give it a moment of silence
you will find that hope is a real
chatterbox

it won't stop talking to you
once you let it get started

hope is everywhere
  even in places where
you won't expect to find it

~ it's in your blood
~ it's in your wrinkles
~ it's in your grief

hope is relentless
amid the noise of
this clanging world

just listen

I swear,
my love,

if you just listen
to the noiseless hope
that surrounds you

I swear

you'll never give up again

John Roedel

#37

love is a ball of
endless yarn that
each of us agrees to
tie an end of it

gently around our fingers

so that when we get separated
from one another

by either the miles, memory

or our mortality

we can tug on
our connection
ever so softly to
send each other
messages back and forth
through the slack

as if to say:

"My love, I'm still here."

"My love, we are endless."

"My love, I can't wait to see you again."

you see,

the connections we make
here on Earth are the most
consecrated of threads

they are the most
unbreakable of blessings

that transform the space that
exists between the people we love

John Roedel

Upon Departure

into a field of divine strings
pulling back and forth on each other

~ it's a stretching symphony of
synchronized tufts of affection

~ it's a spider silk
of stretching
heartfelt vows

~ it's a reaching quid pro quo
of the most tender exchanges

my string-pulling
to those loved ones
I've been separated
From often says:

"my, love, nothing will
ever come between us

nothing

let us be like
two kites forever
entangled in mid-air

I am not bound
to the soil

but to
your soul

~we are tethered
together
like dancing angels
above the tree line

oh, hold my string
and I'll hold yours

John Roedel

and there will
nothing
that can ever
keep us apart"

you see,

~love is a string
tied between two
people

that holds
them together
forever

it's all such a miracle

and I swear that
I'll never let go of my end

and when the moon
comes out tonight to
paint her pale insomnia
on my eyelids

I'll use that sleepless time
to tug on our shared string
we have wrapped around
our fingers as if to say to you:

"Goodnight, my love."

and then I'll hold my
breath until I feel you
pull back on our string
as if you were saying to me:

"Good night, Our love is eternal."

John Roedel

#38

my politics
are the least
interesting thing
about me

I'll be disappointed if

the angel who
scoops me off
of my quiet
deathbed

asks me who I voted for

instead, I hope
my exit interview
consists of only
one question

"Did you heal more than you hurt?"

~ because those are my politics

John Roedel

#39

(dedicated to the memory of Santa Heinemann)

~ if this is to be my final poem

let it be this ~

on my last day
here on Earth

let me be exactly like I
was on my very first

let me be

ready for my
great voyage
between worlds

let me be

ready to ride
the cosmic river
of the vast unknown

on my last day
here on Earth

let me be like I
was on my very first

let me be

ready to see what
all the fuss is on
the other side of
the womb that I've been
hearing so much about

let me be

John Roedel

ready to be bathed in
a light that I could have
never have imagined

let me be

ready to be held in
the arms by my lovely
creator and to feel safer
than I ever have before

on my last day
here on Earth

let me be as I
was on my very first

let me be

ready to see the smiling faces
of all those who have been
eagerly waiting to meet me

let me be

ready to be swaddled up
in the warmest cotton
blanket of fresh starts

on my last day
here on Earth

let me be like
I was on my very first

covered in the
miracle of creation

~no wonder newborn
babies cry

~no wonder 45-year old

John Roedel

men cry

it's all such an adventure
it's all such a journey
it's all such a circle
it's all such a flowing river
it's all such an endless passage
it's all such a mystery

and it goes on and on and on
and on and on

it all goes on

and we go on and on and on
and on and on

we all go on

oh, divine light
oh, sacred spirit

oh, God

if this is to be my last day on Earth
if this is to be my final poem

please let me

go on and on and on
and on and on

oh, I can't wait to see
what comes next

John Roedel

#40
The SuperBloom

death is the wildfire
that rips through
the forest of our life

it scorches the ground
it chars the rocks
it engulfs the trees

death is the fire
that comes to consume
everything

~ but it can't

because after the fire is gone
there is always a miracle waiting
under the ashes of what our lives
used to look like

~ and the miracle is called grief

grief is the slow motion
recovery
that follows the insatiable
fire of death

to grieve the
loss of our beloved

means that death
didn't burn everything

our adoration and memories
of our beloved remain fully
intact underneath the soot
after death rages through

you see,
my love,

John Roedel

death may knock
down every tree
in our forest

but since

grief is the aching itch
of recovery that
we can feel stirring
beneath the scalded ground

it means that death
doesn't get the last word

~ love does

love is the sapling
that come after the
devastating fire

love is the grass pushing
up through the once barren
fire-licked woodland floor

love is relentless
and there is no element
in existence that can
ever destroy it

love is always working
it's way back to us
no matter how hot
the wildfire blazed

grief is proof
that we didn't
let death win

death wants us
to feel numb

John Roedel

~ to feel utter despair

but when we allow
ourselves to grieve

we keep the ashes
from hardening

grief is the fluttering
inside of us that
reminds the world
that although our
world has burned
down to the roots

that there is still
life within us

and if we can hold
on long enough

life will eventually start pouring
out of all of our smoldering wounds

ecologists say that sometimes
when forests burn down
they can explode into thousands
of wildflowers

they call it a "superbloom"

~ that's what grief is

death may burn our world
but grief allows it to grow back

maybe it will never
look like it used to

~ and maybe that is totally okay

because maybe

John Roedel

just maybe

~ grief is meant to change us

grief is the superbloom
that comes after the inferno

John Roedel

Epilogue

"I must be dreaming," I whispered to myself.

I'm walking
barefoot in the snow
around my
small town at night

the storm is growing -
the snowdrifts are building -

the sun is so far away

the only sound
I hear is winter
crunching between
my fat toes

I turn around
and see my
footprints I've
made in the
growing powder

they look smaller
than normal

like the footprints
of a kid

I look down
at my hands

they have shrunk

I touch my face
to discover that
I've shed my wrinkles

I'm a child again

John Roedel

"I must be dreaming."

after walking for a while
I become lost in the snowstorm

I make it to a park
I've never seen before

there are trees with
frozen faces on them

and a patch of luminous
green flowers pushing up
through the blanket of snow

and in the middle
of the park there is
a short bench next to
a tall statue of an angel
playing a bass guitar

this place looks ancient
this place feels brand new

this place is a garden
of contradictions

I trudge over to the bench
and sit down

although I'm somehow not cold
- I start to worry

the storm is raging
and I'm so lost

I sit on the bench
for hours

waiting for a sunrise
that decided to sleep in

John Roedel

I hear crunching in
the snow to my right

and through the blowing snow
I see him

it's my dad
but it's not my dad

he's a barefoot child too

"Hello Jaybird," he says while
waving his small hand

I forgot that's what he
always called me

I was his Jaybird....

"Hello," I reply

my child-aged father sits down
next to me on the tiny bench

we are squeezed tight together

"are you lost, too?" I ask him

"no," he replies. "I'm right where
I'm supposed to be."

the snow is piling
up around us now

my feet are buried

"where are we?" I ask

"we are in the great storm," he says

"how did we get here?"

John Roedel

"I don't know - it's all such
a great mystery, isn't it?"

we sat in silence for an hour
as the snowdrifts rise around us

"I'm so scared," I finally say

"I know Jaybird," he replies as he slips his small fingers through mine

"what do we do now?" I ask

"now we wait for the inevitable glory that comes whenever a great storm ends," he responds

"but what if it doesn't?" I inquire

"all storms end," he says softly

another hour passes
the snow is up to our necks

we are almost snowmen

~ when I hear it

the first-morning song
of a robin

it sounds like a hymn

"there," my dad says "it's happening."

the sun peeks over the eastern
lip of the horizon

and the storm retreats
and the snow begins to melt
and the glory begins

John Roedel

the snow pours off of us
to reveal we aren't
children any more

~we are men
we are sons
~we are fathers

we share the same wrinkles

our fingers still wrapped around
each other's hands

"I must be dreaming," I whisper

"maybe we both are Jaybird," he replies.

we both fight to stay asleep
and enjoy the sunrise and
hymns and glory together

my late father
was right on time

it's all such a great mystery, isn't it?

John Roedel

About the Author

John Roedel is an improv comedic who "stumbled" into writing a few years ago as his life began to fall apart all around him. During his dark night of the soul, John began to have fake conversations with "God" on Facebook to poke fun at his spiritual and personal crisis.

What began as a flippant way of making light of his doubts in the Divine turned into something he wasn't at all prepared for: God wrote back.

Since creating the popular "Hey God. Hey John." blog on Facebook three years ago, John has tackled such topics as his journey to mental health wellness, his lack of faith, the joy and pain of raising a child with autism, and grief, all in the form of a simple conversation with "God."

Eventually, these conversations transformed straight into poetry that has touched hundreds of thousands of people all around the world.

John's newest book "Remedy" was an Amazon bestseller for poetry for five months following its release in November of 2021.

For more information on John Roedel please visit his website at johnroedel.com

John Roedel

Printed in Great Britain
by Amazon